Let The

Adventures

Begin

RETIREMENT
Bucket List Journal

GRENE WATERS
Publishing

The Escapades Of

_____

Retirement is a time to do what you want when you want. You have a whole new life ahead of you. Live it to its' fullest. For life is not meant to be lived sitting on a couch.

And So

Insert Photo Here

My
Adventures
Begin

Congratulations on your retirement!

Now is the time to fulfill your dreams.
Go. Do. Explore. Discover.

This book is all about acquiring memories and experiences during your retirement, not things. Because at the end of the day, it is the memories and feelings that we cherish the most and love to relive.

How many times have you told stories of things in the past which brought back good feelings & laughs and lots of smiles? Well, this book is meant to fill your retirement life with an abundance of those good feelings, memories, laughs and smiles. You only live once so get out there and experience life and live out your dreams. Go. Do. Explore. Discover.

This book is composed of 4 parts:

Part 1 is a list of 125 ideas to inspire you and give you ideas on what you may want to add to your own bucket list. You can use all or you can use none. This list is just a stepping stone for you to think about and discover your own personal dreams and goals.

Part 2 is pages where you can brainstorm your own ideas and make lists of where and what you may want to do. They are not written in stone but it will get the juices flowing and help you set your bucket list goals.

Part 3 is the Master List of all your bucket list items. Here you can easily list your activities and then find those adventures in the future. Because you will want to relive those adventures in the future. Trust us on this.

And Part 4 is the meat of this book. A full page dedicated to each bucket list item. Here you can record the date you nailed it, your story, your best memories, rate your experience, discuss whether it lived up to your expectations and more.

So start dreaming and start making those dreams a reality - because the adventures have only just begun!

Happy Dreaming and Exploring,
Rylee and Jim Waterman
Founders, Grene Waters Publishing

BUCKET LIST INSPIRATION

Family/Friends Ideas:

1. Have a multigenerational family portrait done
2. Host a family reunion
3. Spend a day alone with each child/grandchild/niece, etc.
4. Create your family tree
5. Write about your life/special memories and share it
6. Write a letter to each special person in your life
7. Reconnect with a long lost friend
8. Get together with childhood friends
9. Renew your wedding vows
10. Create a family photo album
11. Create a photo album of your life
12. Begin a new tradition with your family
13. Revisit your honeymoon location
14. Go on a trip with your family/special friends
15. Throw a surprise party for someone you love
16. Revisit your childhood town

Volunteer/Charity Ideas:

17. Volunteer regularly at a non profit in your community
18. Go on an international volunteer trip
19. Become a docent or tour guide
20. Foster pets until they find a permanent home
21. Organize a donation drive in your community
22. Start a little free library in a neighborhood
23. Organize a food drive in your community
24. Become a mentor to a youth in need
25. Become a tutor online or in person

Travel Ideas:

26. See the northern lights in Alaska or Scandinavia
27. Scuba/snorkel the Great Barrier Reef
28. Walk on the Great Wall of China
29. See the Taj Mahal, India
30. Roll the dice in Las Vegas, Nevada
31. Hike/visit the Grand Canyon
32. Ride on the Orient Express
33. Hike the Inca trail to Machu Picchu, Peru
34. Drive Route 66
35. Go on a safari
36. Visit Petra, Jordan
37. Visit the 7 wonders of the ancient world
38. Visit the 7 wonders of the new world
39. See the Great Pyramids of Egypt
40. Go on a cruise
41. Take a tour of the White House in DC
42. Go on a European river cruise
43. Taste wines in Napa Valley, California
44. Go to the top of the Eiffel Tower
45. Visit the Amazon
46. Drive the Pacific Coast Highway, CA
47. Give alms to the monks in Laos
48. Ride a gondola in Venice
49. Visit the Guinness Brewery in Dublin
50. Walk across the Brooklyn Bridge in NY

Travel Ideas (Continued):

51. Take a boat ride on the Mekong River
52. See the Hoodoos in Bryce Canyon National Park, Utah
53. Hike a portion of the Appalachian Trail
54. Visit Mount Rushmore, South Dakota
55. See the changing of the guards in London
56. See a performance in the Opera House in Sydney, Australia
57. Climb up a Mayan ruin in Mexico
58. Explore the Everglades in Florida on an airboat
59. Ride on a trolley in San Francisco
60. See the Lipizzaner horses in Vienna, Austria
61. Ride the Trans-Siberian railway
62. Explore Patagonia in Chile or Argentina
63. Ride on the Maid of the Mist at Niagara Falls, NY
64. Eat and drink your way through Tuscany, Italy
65. Rent a camper van in New Zealand
66. Walk on the Salt Flat in Bolivia
67. Sail around the Greek Islands
68. Sip a cocktail on a beach in the Caribbean
69. Get lost in the alleyways of Fez, Morocco
70. Rent a rowboat on Lago di Braies in the Dolomites, Italy
71. See Victoria Falls between between Zambia and Zimbabwe
72. Visit the Terracotta Army in Xian, China
73. Take a cross country trip
74. Meander through the Grand Bazaar of Istanbul, Turkey
75. Be amazed at Angkor Wat, Cambodia

Adventure Ideas

76. Go skydiving
77. Go paragliding
78. Get your scuba certification
79. Go ziplining
80. Go bungee jumping
81. Dive in a shark cage
82. Swim with the manatees
83. Take a scenic helicopter ride
84. Cross a swinging bridge
85. Go on a hot air balloon ride
86. Sleep in an underwater hotel
87. Eat in an underwater restaurant
88. Travel to Antarctica and sleep under the stars
89. Hike a volcano
90. Snorkel with whalesharks
91. Go on a whale watching cruise
92. Go dog sledding
93. Go white water rafting
94. Canoe/kayak and camp overnight
95. Hike to Base Camp at Mt. Everest
96. Charter a sailboat
97. Hike Mt. Kilimanjaro, Tanzania
98. Go kitesurfing
99. Sleep in an ice hotel
100. Ride in a seaplane
101. Stay in an overwater bungalow

Festivals/Events Ideas

102. Drink beer at Oktoberfest in Munich

102. Attend all the Triple Crown races

103. Celebrate Mardi Gras in New Orleans or Carnival in Rio

104. See a Broadway play in New York

105. Go to the Montreal International Jazz Festival

106. Attend the Indy 500

107. Watch the ball drop on New Years Eve in Times Square

108. Experience Dia de Los Muertos in Mexico

109. Watch the running of the bulls in Pamplona, Spain

110. Go to a World Cup game

111. Experience the Lantern Festival in Thailand

112. Visit the Netherlands during tulip season

113. Attend the Holi festival in India, Nepal or Pakistan

114. See the animal migration in Africa

115. Go to the hot air balloon festival in Albuquerque

116. Go to the championship game of the MLB, NBA or NHL

117. Chill out at the Harbin Ice & Snow Festival in China

118. Throw some tomatoes at La Tomatina in Valencia, Spain

119. Attend the Songkran Festival in Thailand

120. Experience St. Patrick's Day in Dublin, Ireland

121. Attend the Fes Festival in Morocco

122. Experience the Ouidah Int'l Voodoo Festival in Benin

123. Attend the Mevlana Festival (Whirling Dervishes) in Turkey

124. Experience Semana Santa in Spain or Latin America

125. Go to the Vesak Festival in Sri Lanka

BRAINSTORMING

Grab a drink, settle in and start dreaming and planning!

My top wish list of places to visit in the country:

My top wish list of places to visit outside the country:

BRAINSTORMING

Activities I want to experience (skydiving, scuba, etc.):

Special events or festivals I want to attend:

BRAINSTORMING

Skills I would like to acquire or develop:

_____   _____
_____   _____
_____   _____
_____   _____
_____   _____
_____   _____
_____   _____
_____   _____

Things I would like to do with my family or in my community:

_____   _____
_____   _____
_____   _____
_____   _____
_____   _____
_____   _____
_____   _____
_____   _____

Bucket List Notes

The Master List

	Bucket List Item	✓ Off The List
1		
2		
3		
4		
5		
6		
7		
8		
9		
10		
11		
12		
13		
14		
15		
16		
17		
18		
19		
20		
21		
22		
23		

The Master List

	Bucket List Item	✓ Off The List
24		
25		
26		
27		
28		
29		
30		
31		
32		
33		
34		
35		
36		
37		
38		
39		
40		
41		
42		
43		
44		
45		
46		

The Master List

	Bucket List Item	✓ Off The List
47		
48		
49		
50		
51		
52		
53		
54		
55		
56		
57		
58		
59		
60		
61		
62		
63		
64		
65		
66		
67		
68		
69		

The Master List

	Bucket List Item	✓ Off The List
70		
71		
72		
73		
74		
75		
76		
77		
78		
79		
80		
81		
82		
83		
84		
85		
86		
86		
87		
88		
89		
90		
91		

The Master List

	Bucket List Item	✓ Off The List
92		
93		
94		
95		
96		
97		
98		
99		
100		

Notes

01

BUCKET LIST ITEM

_____

_____

I want to do this because

_____

──────── I CAN CHECK IT OFF THE LIST! ────────

The date I nailed it _____

Where the magic happened _____

The Story _____

_____

_____

_____

_____

_____

_____

_____

My Best Memories _____

_____

_____

_____

Did it live up to my expectations? 👍 👎 Why? _____

_____

_____

My overall rating ☀ ☀ ☀ ☀ ☀ Do it again? 👍 👎

02

BUCKET LIST ITEM

_____
_____

I want to do this because

_____
_____

───── I CAN CHECK IT OFF THE LIST! ─────

The date I nailed it _____

Where the magic happened _____

The Story _____

_____

_____

_____

_____

_____

_____

_____

My Best Memories _____

_____

_____

_____

Did it live up to my expectations? 👍 👎 Why?_____

_____

My overall rating ☀ ☀ ☀ ☀ ☀ Do it again? 👍 👎

03

BUCKET LIST ITEM

_____

_____

I want to do this because

_____

——— I CAN CHECK IT OFF THE LIST! ———

The date I nailed it _____

Where the magic happened _____

The Story _____

_____

_____

_____

_____

_____

_____

_____

_____

My Best Memories _____

_____

_____

_____

Did it live up to my expectations? 👍 👎 Why? _____

_____

_____

My overall rating ☀ ☀ ☀ ☀ ☀ Do it again? 👍 👎

04

BUCKET LIST ITEM

_____

_____

I want to do this because

_____

_____

—— I CAN CHECK IT OFF THE LIST! ——

The date I nailed it _____

Where the magic happened _____

The Story _____

_____

_____

_____

_____

_____

_____

_____

_____

My Best Memories _____

_____

_____

_____

Did it live up to my expectations? 👍 👎 Why?_____

_____

_____

My overall rating ☀ ☀ ☀ ☀ ☀ Do it again? 👍 👎

05

BUCKET LIST ITEM

_____
_____

I want to do this because

_____
_____

────── I CAN CHECK IT OFF THE LIST! ──────

The date I nailed it _____

Where the magic happened _____

The Story _____
_____
_____
_____
_____
_____
_____
_____

My Best Memories _____
_____
_____
_____

Did it live up to my expectations? 👍 👎 Why?_____

_____

My overall rating ☀ ☀ ☀ ☀ ☀ Do it again? 👍 👎

06

BUCKET LIST ITEM

_____
_____

I want to do this because

_____

—— I CAN CHECK IT OFF THE LIST! ——

The date I nailed it _____

Where the magic happened _____

The Story _____

_____
_____
_____
_____
_____
_____
_____
_____

My Best Memories _____

_____
_____
_____

Did it live up to my expectations? 👍 👎 Why?_____

_____
_____

My overall rating ☀ ☀ ☀ ☀ ☀ Do it again? 👍 👎

07

BUCKET LIST ITEM

_____
_____

I want to do this because
_____

——— I CAN CHECK IT OFF THE LIST! ———

The date I nailed it _____

Where the magic happened _____

The Story _____
_____
_____
_____
_____
_____
_____
_____
_____

My Best Memories _____
_____
_____
_____

Did it live up to my expectations? 👍 👎 Why? _____
_____

My overall rating ☀ ☀ ☀ ☀ ☀ Do it again? 👍 👎

08

BUCKET LIST ITEM

_____

_____

I want to do this because

_____

_____

———— I CAN CHECK IT OFF THE LIST! ————

The date I nailed it _____

Where the magic happened _____

The Story _____

_____

_____

_____

_____

_____

_____

_____

_____

My Best Memories _____

_____

_____

_____

_____

Did it live up to my expectations? 👍 👎 Why? _____

_____

My overall rating ☀ ☀ ☀ ☀ ☀ Do it again? 👍 👎

09

BUCKET LIST ITEM

_____

_____

I want to do this because

_____

_____

——— I CAN CHECK IT OFF THE LIST! ———

The date I nailed it _____

Where the magic happened _____

The Story _____

_____

_____

_____

_____

_____

_____

_____

My Best Memories _____

_____

_____

_____

_____

Did it live up to my expectations? 👍 👎 Why? _____

_____

_____

My overall rating ☀ ☀ ☀ ☀ ☀ Do it again? 👍 👎

10

BUCKET LIST ITEM

_____

_____

I want to do this because

_____

_____

——— I CAN CHECK IT OFF THE LIST! ———

The date I nailed it _____

Where the magic happened _____

The Story _____

_____

_____

_____

_____

_____

_____

_____

_____

_____

My Best Memories _____

_____

_____

_____

_____

Did it live up to my expectations? 👍 👎 Why?_____

_____

_____

My overall rating ☀ ☀ ☀ ☀ ☀ Do it again? 👍 👎

11

BUCKET LIST ITEM

_____

_____

I want to do this because

_____

_____

—— I CAN CHECK IT OFF THE LIST! ——

The date I nailed it _____

Where the magic happened _____

The Story _____

_____

_____

_____

_____

_____

_____

_____

_____

My Best Memories _____

_____

_____

_____

Did it live up to my expectations? 👍 👎 Why?_____

_____

_____

My overall rating ☀ ☀ ☀ ☀ ☀ Do it again? 👍 👎

12

BUCKET LIST ITEM

_____

_____

I want to do this because

_____

_____

— **I CAN CHECK IT OFF THE LIST!** —

The date I nailed it _____

Where the magic happened _____

The Story _____

_____

_____

_____

_____

_____

_____

_____

_____

My Best Memories _____

_____

_____

_____

_____

Did it live up to my expectations? 👍 👎 Why?_____

_____

_____

My overall rating ☀ ☀ ☀ ☀ ☀ Do it again? 👍 👎

13

BUCKET LIST ITEM

_____

_____

I want to do this because

_____

_____

—————— I CAN CHECK IT OFF THE LIST! ——————

The date I nailed it _____

Where the magic happened _____

The Story _____

_____

_____

_____

_____

_____

_____

_____

_____

My Best Memories _____

_____

_____

_____

_____

Did it live up to my expectations? 👍 👎 Why?_____

_____

My overall rating ☀ ☀ ☀ ☀ ☀ Do it again? 👍 👎

14

BUCKET LIST ITEM

_____

_____

I want to do this because

_____

_____

——— I CAN CHECK IT OFF THE LIST! ———

The date I nailed it _____

Where the magic happened _____

The Story _____

_____

_____

_____

_____

_____

_____

_____

_____

My Best Memories _____

_____

_____

_____

Did it live up to my expectations? 👍 👎 Why? _____

_____

_____

My overall rating ☀ ☀ ☀ ☀ ☀ Do it again? 👍 👎

15

BUCKET LIST ITEM

_____
_____

I want to do this because

_____
_____

——— I CAN CHECK IT OFF THE LIST! ———

The date I nailed it _____

Where the magic happened _____

The Story _____
_____
_____
_____
_____
_____
_____
_____
_____
_____

My Best Memories _____
_____
_____
_____

Did it live up to my expectations? 👍 👎 Why? _____
_____

My overall rating ☀ ☀ ☀ ☀ ☀ Do it again? 👍 👎

16

BUCKET LIST ITEM

_____
_____

I want to do this because

_____
_____

———— I CAN CHECK IT OFF THE LIST! ————

The date I nailed it _____

Where the magic happened _____

The Story _____
_____
_____
_____
_____
_____
_____
_____
_____

My Best Memories _____
_____
_____
_____

Did it live up to my expectations? 👍 👎 Why?_____

_____

My overall rating ☀ ☀ ☀ ☀ ☀ Do it again? 👍 👎

17

BUCKET LIST ITEM

_____
_____

I want to do this because

_____
_____

————— I CAN CHECK IT OFF THE LIST! —————

The date I nailed it _____

Where the magic happened _____

The Story _____
_____
_____
_____
_____
_____
_____
_____
_____

My Best Memories _____
_____
_____
_____

Did it live up to my expectations? 👍 👎 Why?_____
_____
_____

My overall rating ☀ ☀ ☀ ☀ ☀ Do it again? 👍 👎

18

BUCKET LIST ITEM

_____

_____

I want to do this because

_____

—— I CAN CHECK IT OFF THE LIST! ——

The date I nailed it _____

Where the magic happened _____

The Story _____

_____

_____

_____

_____

_____

_____

_____

_____

My Best Memories _____

_____

_____

_____

Did it live up to my expectations? 👍 👎 Why? _____

_____

_____

My overall rating ☀ ☀ ☀ ☀ ☀ Do it again? 👍 👎

19

BUCKET LIST ITEM

_____
_____

I want to do this because

_____

————— I CAN CHECK IT OFF THE LIST! —————

The date I nailed it _____

Where the magic happened _____

The Story _____
_____
_____
_____
_____
_____
_____
_____
_____
_____
_____

My Best Memories _____
_____
_____
_____
_____

Did it live up to my expectations? 👍 👎 Why? _____
_____
_____

My overall rating ☀ ☀ ☀ ☀ ☀ Do it again? 👍 👎

20

BUCKET LIST ITEM

_____

_____

I want to do this because

_____

_____

—————— I CAN CHECK IT OFF THE LIST! ——————

The date I nailed it _____

Where the magic happened _____

The Story _____

_____

_____

_____

_____

_____

_____

_____

_____

My Best Memories _____

_____

_____

_____

_____

Did it live up to my expectations? 👍 👎 Why? _____

_____

_____

My overall rating ☀ ☀ ☀ ☀ ☀ Do it again? 👍 👎

21

BUCKET LIST ITEM

_____

_____

I want to do this because

_____

_____

―――――― I CAN CHECK IT OFF THE LIST! ――――――

The date I nailed it _____

Where the magic happened _____

The Story _____

_____

_____

_____

_____

_____

_____

_____

My Best Memories _____

_____

_____

_____

Did it live up to my expectations? 👍 👎 Why? _____

_____

_____

My overall rating ☀ ☀ ☀ ☀ ☀ Do it again? 👍 👎

22

BUCKET LIST ITEM

_____

_____

I want to do this because

_____

_____

———— I CAN CHECK IT OFF THE LIST! ————

The date I nailed it _____

Where the magic happened _____

The Story _____

_____

_____

_____

_____

_____

_____

_____

_____

My Best Memories _____

_____

_____

_____

Did it live up to my expectations? 👍 👎 Why?_____

_____

_____

My overall rating ☀ ☀ ☀ ☀ ☀ Do it again? 👍 👎

23

BUCKET LIST ITEM

_____
_____

I want to do this because
_____
_____

———— I CAN CHECK IT OFF THE LIST! ————

The date I nailed it _____

Where the magic happened _____

The Story _____
_____
_____
_____
_____
_____
_____
_____
_____
_____

My Best Memories _____
_____
_____
_____

Did it live up to my expectations? 👍 👎 Why? _____
_____
_____

My overall rating ☀ ☀ ☀ ☀ ☀ Do it again? 👍 👎

24

BUCKET LIST ITEM

_____

_____

I want to do this because

_____

_____

—— I CAN CHECK IT OFF THE LIST! ——

The date I nailed it _____

Where the magic happened _____

The Story _____

_____

_____

_____

_____

_____

_____

_____

_____

My Best Memories _____

_____

_____

_____

Did it live up to my expectations? 👍 👎 Why?_____

_____

My overall rating ☀ ☀ ☀ ☀ ☀ Do it again? 👍 👎

25

BUCKET LIST ITEM

_____
_____

I want to do this because

_____
_____

———— I CAN CHECK IT OFF THE LIST! ————

The date I nailed it _____

Where the magic happened _____

The Story _____
_____
_____
_____
_____
_____
_____
_____

My Best Memories _____
_____
_____
_____

Did it live up to my expectations? 👍 👎 Why?_____
_____

My overall rating ☀ ☀ ☀ ☀ ☀ Do it again? 👍 👎

26

BUCKET LIST ITEM

_____

_____

I want to do this because

_____

_____

───── I CAN CHECK IT OFF THE LIST! ─────

The date I nailed it _____

Where the magic happened _____

The Story _____

_____

_____

_____

_____

_____

_____

_____

_____

My Best Memories _____

_____

_____

_____

Did it live up to my expectations? 👍 👎 Why?_____

_____

_____

My overall rating ☀ ☀ ☀ ☀ ☀ Do it again? 👍 👎

27

BUCKET LIST ITEM

_____

_____

I want to do this because

_____

——— I CAN CHECK IT OFF THE LIST! ———

The date I nailed it _____

Where the magic happened _____

The Story _____

_____

_____

_____

_____

_____

_____

_____

_____

My Best Memories _____

_____

_____

_____

Did it live up to my expectations? 👍 👎 Why? _____

_____

_____

My overall rating ☀ ☀ ☀ ☀ ☀ Do it again? 👍 👎

28

BUCKET LIST ITEM

_____
_____

I want to do this because

_____
_____

—————— I CAN CHECK IT OFF THE LIST! ——————

The date I nailed it _____

Where the magic happened _____

The Story _____

_____
_____
_____
_____
_____
_____
_____
_____

My Best Memories _____

_____
_____
_____

Did it live up to my expectations? 👍 👎 Why? _____

_____
_____

My overall rating ☀ ☀ ☀ ☀ ☀ Do it again? 👍 👎

29

BUCKET LIST ITEM

_____
_____

I want to do this because

_____
_____

——— I CAN CHECK IT OFF THE LIST! ———

The date I nailed it _____

Where the magic happened _____

The Story _____
_____
_____
_____
_____
_____
_____
_____
_____

My Best Memories _____
_____
_____
_____

Did it live up to my expectations? 👍 👎 Why? _____
_____
_____

My overall rating ☀ ☀ ☀ ☀ ☀ Do it again? 👍 👎

30

BUCKET LIST ITEM

_____

_____

I want to do this because

_____

_____

———— I CAN CHECK IT OFF THE LIST! ————

The date I nailed it _____

Where the magic happened _____

The Story _____

_____

_____

_____

_____

_____

_____

_____

_____

My Best Memories _____

_____

_____

_____

_____

Did it live up to my expectations? 👍 👎 Why? _____

_____

_____

My overall rating ☀ ☀ ☀ ☀ ☀ Do it again? 👍 👎

31

BUCKET LIST ITEM

_____

_____

I want to do this because

_____

—————— I CAN CHECK IT OFF THE LIST! ——————

The date I nailed it _____

Where the magic happened _____

The Story _____

_____

_____

_____

_____

_____

_____

_____

My Best Memories _____

_____

_____

_____

Did it live up to my expectations? 👍 👎 Why?_____

_____

My overall rating ☀ ☀ ☀ ☀ ☀ Do it again? 👍 👎

32

BUCKET LIST ITEM

_____
_____

I want to do this because
_____

———— I CAN CHECK IT OFF THE LIST! ————

The date I nailed it _____

Where the magic happened _____

The Story _____
_____
_____
_____
_____
_____
_____
_____
_____
_____

My Best Memories _____
_____
_____
_____
_____

Did it live up to my expectations? 👍 👎 Why?_____

_____

My overall rating ☀ ☀ ☀ ☀ ☀ Do it again? 👍 👎

33

BUCKET LIST ITEM

_____

_____

I want to do this because

_____

_____

——— I CAN CHECK IT OFF THE LIST! ———

The date I nailed it _____

Where the magic happened _____

The Story _____

_____

_____

_____

_____

_____

_____

_____

My Best Memories _____

_____

_____

_____

Did it live up to my expectations? 👍 👎 Why?_____

_____

_____

My overall rating ☀ ☀ ☀ ☀ ☀ Do it again? 👍 👎

34

BUCKET LIST ITEM

_____
_____

I want to do this because
_____

_____

———— I CAN CHECK IT OFF THE LIST! ————

The date I nailed it _____

Where the magic happened _____

The Story _____

_____

_____

_____

_____

_____

_____

_____

_____

_____

My Best Memories _____

_____

_____

_____

Did it live up to my expectations? 👍 👎 Why?_____

_____

_____

My overall rating ☀ ☀ ☀ ☀ ☀ Do it again? 👍 👎

35

BUCKET LIST ITEM

_____
_____
_____

I want to do this because

_____
_____

—— I CAN CHECK IT OFF THE LIST! ——

The date I nailed it _____

Where the magic happened _____

The Story _____
_____
_____
_____
_____
_____
_____
_____
_____

My Best Memories _____
_____
_____
_____

Did it live up to my expectations? 👍 👎 Why?_____
_____
_____

My overall rating ☀ ☀ ☀ ☀ ☀ Do it again? 👍 👎

36

BUCKET LIST ITEM

_____

_____

I want to do this because

_____

_____

— I CAN CHECK IT OFF THE LIST! —

The date I nailed it _____

Where the magic happened _____

The Story _____

_____

_____

_____

_____

_____

_____

_____

_____

My Best Memories _____

_____

_____

_____

Did it live up to my expectations? 👍 👎 Why? _____

_____

My overall rating ☀ ☀ ☀ ☀ ☀ Do it again? 👍 👎

37

BUCKET LIST ITEM

_____

_____

I want to do this because

_____

_____

—————— I CAN CHECK IT OFF THE LIST! ——————

The date I nailed it _____

Where the magic happened _____

The Story _____

_____

_____

_____

_____

_____

_____

_____

My Best Memories _____

_____

_____

_____

Did it live up to my expectations? 👍 👎 Why?_____

_____

My overall rating ☀ ☀ ☀ ☀ ☀ Do it again? 👍 👎

38

BUCKET LIST ITEM

_____
_____

I want to do this because
_____
_____

—— I CAN CHECK IT OFF THE LIST! ——

The date I nailed it _____

Where the magic happened _____

The Story _____
_____
_____
_____
_____
_____
_____
_____
_____
_____

My Best Memories _____
_____
_____
_____
_____

Did it live up to my expectations? 👍 👎 Why?_____
_____
_____

My overall rating ☀ ☀ ☀ ☀ ☀ Do it again? 👍 👎

39

BUCKET LIST ITEM

_____

_____

I want to do this because

_____

_____

——— I CAN CHECK IT OFF THE LIST! ———

The date I nailed it _____

Where the magic happened _____

The Story _____

_____

_____

_____

_____

_____

_____

_____

My Best Memories _____

_____

_____

_____

Did it live up to my expectations? 👍 👎 Why?_____

_____

My overall rating ☀ ☀ ☀ ☀ ☀ Do it again? 👍 👎

40

BUCKET LIST ITEM

_____

_____

I want to do this because

_____

_____

——— I CAN CHECK IT OFF THE LIST! ———

The date I nailed it _____

Where the magic happened _____

The Story _____

_____

_____

_____

_____

_____

_____

_____

_____

_____

My Best Memories _____

_____

_____

_____

Did it live up to my expectations? 👍 👎 Why? _____

_____

_____

My overall rating ☀ ☀ ☀ ☀ ☀ Do it again? 👍 👎

41

BUCKET LIST ITEM

_____

_____

I want to do this because

_____

_____

—— I CAN CHECK IT OFF THE LIST! ——

The date I nailed it _____

Where the magic happened _____

The Story _____

_____

_____

_____

_____

_____

_____

_____

My Best Memories _____

_____

_____

_____

Did it live up to my expectations? 👍 👎 Why? _____

_____

_____

My overall rating ☀ ☀ ☀ ☀ ☀ Do it again? 👍 👎

42

BUCKET LIST ITEM

_____
_____

I want to do this because
_____

_____

———— I CAN CHECK IT OFF THE LIST! ————

The date I nailed it _____

Where the magic happened _____

The Story _____
_____
_____
_____
_____
_____
_____
_____
_____
_____
_____

My Best Memories _____
_____
_____
_____
_____

Did it live up to my expectations? 👍 👎 Why?_____

_____
_____

My overall rating ☀ ☀ ☀ ☀ ☀ Do it again? 👍 👎

43

BUCKET LIST ITEM

_____
_____

I want to do this because
_____
_____

——— I CAN CHECK IT OFF THE LIST! ———

The date I nailed it _____

Where the magic happened _____

The Story _____
_____
_____
_____
_____
_____
_____
_____
_____

My Best Memories _____
_____
_____
_____

Did it live up to my expectations? 👍 👎 Why? _____
_____
_____

My overall rating ☀ ☀ ☀ ☀ ☀ Do it again? 👍 👎

44

BUCKET LIST ITEM

_____
_____

I want to do this because

_____

──── I CAN CHECK IT OFF THE LIST! ────

The date I nailed it _____

Where the magic happened _____

The Story _____
_____
_____
_____
_____
_____
_____
_____
_____

My Best Memories _____
_____
_____
_____
_____

Did it live up to my expectations? 👍 👎 Why? _____

_____
_____

My overall rating ☀ ☀ ☀ ☀ ☀ Do it again? 👍 👎

45

BUCKET LIST ITEM

_____

_____

I want to do this because

_____

_____

———— I CAN CHECK IT OFF THE LIST! ————

The date I nailed it _____

Where the magic happened _____

The Story _____

_____

_____

_____

_____

_____

_____

_____

My Best Memories _____

_____

_____

_____

Did it live up to my expectations? 👍 👎 Why? _____

_____

My overall rating ☀ ☀ ☀ ☀ ☀ Do it again? 👍 👎

46

BUCKET LIST ITEM

_____
_____

I want to do this because
_____

_____

——— I CAN CHECK IT OFF THE LIST! ———

The date I nailed it _____

Where the magic happened _____

The Story _____
_____
_____
_____
_____
_____
_____
_____
_____
_____
_____

My Best Memories _____
_____
_____
_____

Did it live up to my expectations? 👍 👎 Why? _____
_____
_____

My overall rating ☀ ☀ ☀ ☀ ☀ Do it again? 👍 👎

47

BUCKET LIST ITEM

_____

_____

I want to do this because

_____

_____

———— I CAN CHECK IT OFF THE LIST! ————

The date I nailed it _____

Where the magic happened _____

The Story _____

_____

_____

_____

_____

_____

_____

_____

_____

My Best Memories _____

_____

_____

_____

Did it live up to my expectations? 👍 👎 Why? _____

_____

My overall rating ☀ ☀ ☀ ☀ ☀ Do it again? 👍 👎

48

BUCKET LIST ITEM

_____

_____

I want to do this because

_____

_____

—— I CAN CHECK IT OFF THE LIST! ——

The date I nailed it _____

Where the magic happened _____

The Story _____

_____

_____

_____

_____

_____

_____

_____

_____

My Best Memories _____

_____

_____

_____

Did it live up to my expectations? 👍 👎 Why? _____

_____

_____

My overall rating ☀ ☀ ☀ ☀ ☀ Do it again? 👍 👎

49

BUCKET LIST ITEM

_____

_____

I want to do this because

_____

_____

—— I CAN CHECK IT OFF THE LIST! ——

The date I nailed it _____

Where the magic happened _____

The Story _____

_____

_____

_____

_____

_____

_____

_____

My Best Memories _____

_____

_____

_____

_____

Did it live up to my expectations? 👍 👎 Why? _____

_____

_____

My overall rating ☀ ☀ ☀ ☀ ☀ Do it again? 👍 👎

50

BUCKET LIST ITEM

_____

_____

I want to do this because

_____

—— I CAN CHECK IT OFF THE LIST! ——

The date I nailed it _____

Where the magic happened _____

The Story _____

_____

_____

_____

_____

_____

_____

_____

_____

_____

My Best Memories _____

_____

_____

_____

Did it live up to my expectations? 👍 👎 Why?_____

_____

_____

My overall rating ☀ ☀ ☀ ☀ ☀ Do it again? 👍 👎

51

BUCKET LIST ITEM

_____

_____

I want to do this because

_____

———— I CAN CHECK IT OFF THE LIST! ————

The date I nailed it _____

Where the magic happened _____

The Story _____

_____

_____

_____

_____

_____

_____

_____

_____

My Best Memories _____

_____

_____

_____

Did it live up to my expectations? 👍 👎 Why?_____

_____

_____

My overall rating ☀ ☀ ☀ ☀ ☀ Do it again? 👍 👎

52

BUCKET LIST ITEM

_____

_____

I want to do this because

_____

_____

————— I CAN CHECK IT OFF THE LIST! —————

The date I nailed it _____

Where the magic happened _____

The Story _____

_____

_____

_____

_____

_____

_____

_____

_____

My Best Memories _____

_____

_____

_____

_____

Did it live up to my expectations? 👍 👎 Why?_____

_____

_____

My overall rating ☀ ☀ ☀ ☀ ☀ Do it again? 👍 👎

53

BUCKET LIST ITEM

_____

_____

I want to do this because

_____

_____

———— I CAN CHECK IT OFF THE LIST! ————

The date I nailed it _____

Where the magic happened _____

The Story _____

_____

_____

_____

_____

_____

_____

_____

_____

My Best Memories _____

_____

_____

_____

Did it live up to my expectations? 👍 👎 Why?_____

_____

My overall rating ☀ ☀ ☀ ☀ ☀ Do it again? 👍 👎

54

BUCKET LIST ITEM
_____
_____

I want to do this because
_____

———— I CAN CHECK IT OFF THE LIST! ————

The date I nailed it _____

Where the magic happened _____

The Story _____
_____
_____
_____
_____
_____
_____
_____
_____
_____
_____

My Best Memories _____
_____
_____
_____

Did it live up to my expectations? 👍 👎 Why? _____
_____
_____

My overall rating ☀ ☀ ☀ ☀ ☀ Do it again? 👍 👎

55

BUCKET LIST ITEM

_____
_____

I want to do this because

_____

—— I CAN CHECK IT OFF THE LIST! ——

The date I nailed it _____

Where the magic happened _____

The Story _____
_____
_____
_____
_____
_____
_____
_____
_____

My Best Memories _____
_____
_____
_____

Did it live up to my expectations? 👍 👎 Why?_____

_____

My overall rating ☀ ☀ ☀ ☀ ☀ Do it again? 👍 👎

56

BUCKET LIST ITEM

_____

_____

I want to do this because

_____

_____

────── I CAN CHECK IT OFF THE LIST! ──────

The date I nailed it _____

Where the magic happened _____

The Story _____

_____

_____

_____

_____

_____

_____

_____

_____

_____

My Best Memories _____

_____

_____

_____

_____

Did it live up to my expectations? 👍 👎 Why?_____

_____

_____

My overall rating ☀ ☀ ☀ ☀ ☀ Do it again?

57

BUCKET LIST ITEM

_____

_____

I want to do this because

_____

_____

— I CAN CHECK IT OFF THE LIST! —

The date I nailed it _____

Where the magic happened _____

The Story _____

_____

_____

_____

_____

_____

_____

_____

My Best Memories _____

_____

_____

_____

Did it live up to my expectations? 👍 👎 Why?_____

_____

My overall rating ☀ ☀ ☀ ☀ ☀ Do it again? 👍 👎

58

BUCKET LIST ITEM

_____
_____

I want to do this because

_____
_____

——— I CAN CHECK IT OFF THE LIST! ———

The date I nailed it _____

Where the magic happened _____

The Story _____
_____
_____
_____
_____
_____
_____
_____
_____
_____
_____

My Best Memories _____
_____
_____
_____
_____

Did it live up to my expectations? 👍 👎 Why?_____

_____

My overall rating ☀ ☀ ☀ ☀ ☀ Do it again? 👍 👎

59

BUCKET LIST ITEM

_____
_____

I want to do this because
_____
_____

───── I CAN CHECK IT OFF THE LIST! ─────

The date I nailed it _____

Where the magic happened _____

The Story _____
_____
_____
_____
_____
_____
_____
_____
_____
_____

My Best Memories _____
_____
_____
_____

Did it live up to my expectations? 👍 👎 Why?_____
_____
_____

My overall rating ☀ ☀ ☀ ☀ ☀ Do it again? 👍 👎

60

BUCKET LIST ITEM

_____
_____

I want to do this because
_____
_____

—— I CAN CHECK IT OFF THE LIST! ——

The date I nailed it _____

Where the magic happened _____

The Story _____
_____
_____
_____
_____
_____
_____
_____
_____
_____

My Best Memories _____
_____
_____
_____
_____

Did it live up to my expectations? 👍 👎 Why? _____
_____
_____

My overall rating ☀ ☀ ☀ ☀ ☀ Do it again? 👍 👎

61

BUCKET LIST ITEM

_____

_____

I want to do this because

_____

_____

— I CAN CHECK IT OFF THE LIST! —

The date I nailed it _____

Where the magic happened _____

The Story _____

_____

_____

_____

_____

_____

_____

_____

My Best Memories _____

_____

_____

_____

Did it live up to my expectations? 👍 👎 Why? _____

_____

My overall rating ☀ ☀ ☀ ☀ ☀ Do it again? 👍 👎

62

BUCKET LIST ITEM

_____

_____

I want to do this because

_____

———— I CAN CHECK IT OFF THE LIST! ————

The date I nailed it _____

Where the magic happened _____

The Story _____

_____

_____

_____

_____

_____

_____

_____

_____

_____

My Best Memories _____

_____

_____

_____

_____

Did it live up to my expectations? 👍 👎 Why? _____

_____

_____

My overall rating ☀ ☀ ☀ ☀ ☀ Do it again? 👍 👎

63

BUCKET LIST ITEM

_____
_____

I want to do this because

_____
_____

—————— I CAN CHECK IT OFF THE LIST! ——————

The date I nailed it _____

Where the magic happened _____

The Story _____
_____
_____
_____
_____
_____
_____
_____
_____

My Best Memories _____
_____
_____
_____

Did it live up to my expectations? 👍 👎 Why? _____
_____

My overall rating ☀ ☀ ☀ ☀ ☀ Do it again? 👍 👎

64

BUCKET LIST ITEM

_____

_____

I want to do this because

_____

_____

—— I CAN CHECK IT OFF THE LIST! ——

The date I nailed it _____

Where the magic happened _____

The Story _____

_____

_____

_____

_____

_____

_____

_____

_____

My Best Memories _____

_____

_____

_____

Did it live up to my expectations? 👍 👎 Why? _____

_____

_____

My overall rating ☀ ☀ ☀ ☀ ☀ Do it again? 👍 👎

65

BUCKET LIST ITEM

_____

_____

I want to do this because

_____

_____

————— I CAN CHECK IT OFF THE LIST! —————

The date I nailed it _____

Where the magic happened _____

The Story _____

_____

_____

_____

_____

_____

_____

_____

My Best Memories _____

_____

_____

_____

Did it live up to my expectations? 👍 👎 Why?_____

_____

My overall rating ☀ ☀ ☀ ☀ ☀ Do it again? 👍 👎

66

BUCKET LIST ITEM
_____
_____

I want to do this because
_____

——— I CAN CHECK IT OFF THE LIST! ———

The date I nailed it _____

Where the magic happened _____

The Story _____
_____
_____
_____
_____
_____
_____
_____
_____
_____
_____

My Best Memories _____
_____
_____
_____
_____

Did it live up to my expectations? 👍 👎 Why? _____

_____

My overall rating ☀ ☀ ☀ ☀ ☀ Do it again? 👍 👎

67

BUCKET LIST ITEM

_____

_____

I want to do this because

_____

_____

—————— I CAN CHECK IT OFF THE LIST! ——————

The date I nailed it _____

Where the magic happened _____

The Story _____

_____

_____

_____

_____

_____

_____

_____

_____

My Best Memories _____

_____

_____

_____

Did it live up to my expectations? 👍 👎 Why? _____

_____

_____

My overall rating ☀ ☀ ☀ ☀ ☀ Do it again? 👍 👎

68

BUCKET LIST ITEM

_____
_____

I want to do this because

_____
_____

——— I CAN CHECK IT OFF THE LIST! ———

The date I nailed it _____

Where the magic happened _____

The Story _____

_____

_____

_____

_____

_____

_____

_____

My Best Memories _____

_____

_____

_____

_____

Did it live up to my expectations? 👍 👎 Why?_____

_____

_____

My overall rating ☀☀☀☀☀ Do it again? 👍 👎

69

BUCKET LIST ITEM

_____
_____

I want to do this because
_____

———— I CAN CHECK IT OFF THE LIST! ————

The date I nailed it _____

Where the magic happened _____

The Story _____
_____
_____
_____
_____
_____
_____
_____

My Best Memories _____
_____
_____
_____

Did it live up to my expectations? 👍 👎 Why?_____

_____

My overall rating ☀ ☀ ☀ ☀ ☀ Do it again? 👍 👎

70

BUCKET LIST ITEM
_____
_____

I want to do this because
_____
_____

———— I CAN CHECK IT OFF THE LIST! ————

The date I nailed it _____

Where the magic happened _____

The Story _____
_____
_____
_____
_____
_____
_____
_____
_____
_____

My Best Memories _____
_____
_____
_____
_____

Did it live up to my expectations? 👍 👎 Why?_____
_____
_____

My overall rating ☀ ☀ ☀ ☀ ☀ Do it again? 👍 👎

71

BUCKET LIST ITEM

_____

_____

I want to do this because

_____

_____

—————— I CAN CHECK IT OFF THE LIST! ——————

The date I nailed it _____

Where the magic happened _____

The Story _____

_____

_____

_____

_____

_____

_____

_____

_____

My Best Memories _____

_____

_____

_____

Did it live up to my expectations? 👍 👎 Why? _____

_____

_____

My overall rating ☀ ☀ ☀ ☀ ☀ Do it again? 👍 👎

72

BUCKET LIST ITEM

_____
_____

I want to do this because
_____
_____

———— I CAN CHECK IT OFF THE LIST! ————

The date I nailed it _____

Where the magic happened _____

The Story _____
_____
_____
_____
_____
_____
_____
_____
_____
_____

My Best Memories _____
_____
_____
_____
_____

Did it live up to my expectations? 👍 👎 Why? _____
_____

My overall rating ☀ ☀ ☀ ☀ ☀ Do it again? 👍 👎

73

BUCKET LIST ITEM

_____

_____

I want to do this because

_____

_____

——— I CAN CHECK IT OFF THE LIST! ———

The date I nailed it _____

Where the magic happened _____

The Story _____

_____

_____

_____

_____

_____

_____

_____

_____

My Best Memories _____

_____

_____

_____

Did it live up to my expectations? 👍 👎 Why? _____

_____

_____

My overall rating ☀ ☀ ☀ ☀ ☀ Do it again? 👍 👎

74

BUCKET LIST ITEM

_____

_____

I want to do this because

_____

―――――― **I CAN CHECK IT OFF THE LIST!** ――――――

The date I nailed it _____

Where the magic happened _____

The Story _____

_____

_____

_____

_____

_____

_____

_____

_____

_____

My Best Memories _____

_____

_____

_____

_____

Did it live up to my expectations? 👍 👎 Why?_____

_____

_____

My overall rating ☀ ☀ ☀ ☀ ☀ Do it again? 👍 👎

75

BUCKET LIST ITEM

_____
_____

I want to do this because

_____
_____

———— I CAN CHECK IT OFF THE LIST! ————

The date I nailed it _____

Where the magic happened _____

The Story _____
_____
_____
_____
_____
_____
_____
_____
_____

My Best Memories _____
_____
_____
_____

Did it live up to my expectations? 👍 👎 Why? _____
_____
_____

My overall rating ☀ ☀ ☀ ☀ ☀ Do it again? 👍 👎

76

BUCKET LIST ITEM
_____
_____

I want to do this because
_____
_____

————— I CAN CHECK IT OFF THE LIST! —————

The date I nailed it _____

Where the magic happened _____

The Story _____
_____
_____
_____
_____
_____
_____
_____
_____

My Best Memories _____
_____
_____
_____

Did it live up to my expectations? 👍 👎 Why?_____
_____
_____

My overall rating ☀ ☀ ☀ ☀ ☀ Do it again? 👍 👎

77

BUCKET LIST ITEM

_____

_____

I want to do this because

_____

_____

— I CAN CHECK IT OFF THE LIST! —

The date I nailed it _____

Where the magic happened _____

The Story _____

_____

_____

_____

_____

_____

_____

My Best Memories _____

_____

_____

_____

Did it live up to my expectations? 👍 👎 Why? _____

_____

_____

My overall rating ☀ ☀ ☀ ☀ ☀ Do it again? 👍 👎

78

BUCKET LIST ITEM

_____
_____

I want to do this because
_____

———— I CAN CHECK IT OFF THE LIST! ————

The date I nailed it _____

Where the magic happened _____

The Story _____
_____
_____
_____
_____
_____
_____
_____
_____
_____

My Best Memories _____
_____
_____
_____

Did it live up to my expectations? 👍 👎 Why? _____
_____

My overall rating ☀ ☀ ☀ ☀ ☀ Do it again? 👍 👎

79

BUCKET LIST ITEM

_____
_____

I want to do this because
_____
_____

—————— I CAN CHECK IT OFF THE LIST! ——————

The date I nailed it _____

Where the magic happened _____

The Story _____
_____
_____
_____
_____
_____
_____
_____
_____

My Best Memories _____
_____
_____
_____

Did it live up to my expectations? 👍 👎 Why? _____
_____

My overall rating ☀ ☀ ☀ ☀ ☀ Do it again? 👍 👎

80

BUCKET LIST ITEM

_____
_____
_____

I want to do this because

_____
_____

——— I CAN CHECK IT OFF THE LIST! ———

The date I nailed it _____

Where the magic happened _____

The Story _____
_____
_____
_____
_____
_____
_____
_____
_____
_____
_____

My Best Memories _____
_____
_____
_____
_____

Did it live up to my expectations? 👍 👎 Why? _____
_____
_____

My overall rating ☀ ☀ ☀ ☀ ☀ Do it again? 👍 👎

81

BUCKET LIST ITEM

_____

_____

I want to do this because

_____

_____

─── I CAN CHECK IT OFF THE LIST! ───

The date I nailed it _____

Where the magic happened _____

The Story _____

_____

_____

_____

_____

_____

_____

_____

_____

My Best Memories _____

_____

_____

_____

_____

Did it live up to my expectations? 👍 👎 Why? _____

_____

_____

My overall rating ☀ ☀ ☀ ☀ ☀ Do it again? 👍 👎

82

BUCKET LIST ITEM

_____
_____

I want to do this because

_____

————— I CAN CHECK IT OFF THE LIST! —————

The date I nailed it _____

Where the magic happened _____

The Story _____
_____
_____
_____
_____
_____
_____
_____
_____
_____

My Best Memories _____
_____
_____
_____
_____

Did it live up to my expectations? 👍 👎 Why?_____

_____
_____

My overall rating ☀ ☀ ☀ ☀ ☀ Do it again? 👍 👎

83

BUCKET LIST ITEM

_____

_____

I want to do this because

_____

───── I CAN CHECK IT OFF THE LIST! ─────

The date I nailed it _____

Where the magic happened _____

The Story _____

_____

_____

_____

_____

_____

_____

_____

My Best Memories _____

_____

_____

_____

Did it live up to my expectations? 👍 👎 Why? _____

_____

_____

My overall rating ☀ ☀ ☀ ☀ ☀ Do it again? 👍 👎

84

BUCKET LIST ITEM

_____

_____

I want to do this because

_____

——— I CAN CHECK IT OFF THE LIST! ———

The date I nailed it _____

Where the magic happened _____

The Story _____

_____

_____

_____

_____

_____

_____

_____

My Best Memories _____

_____

_____

_____

Did it live up to my expectations? 👍 👎 Why? _____

_____

My overall rating ☀ ☀ ☀ ☀ ☀ Do it again? 👍 👎

85

BUCKET LIST ITEM

_____

_____

I want to do this because

_____

_____

———— I CAN CHECK IT OFF THE LIST! ————

The date I nailed it _____

Where the magic happened _____

The Story _____

_____

_____

_____

_____

_____

_____

_____

My Best Memories _____

_____

_____

_____

Did it live up to my expectations? 👍 👎 Why?_____

_____

My overall rating ☀ ☀ ☀ ☀ ☀ Do it again? 👍 👎

86

BUCKET LIST ITEM

_____

_____

I want to do this because

_____

—————— I CAN CHECK IT OFF THE LIST! ——————

The date I nailed it _____

Where the magic happened _____

The Story _____

_____

_____

_____

_____

_____

_____

_____

_____

_____

My Best Memories _____

_____

_____

_____

_____

Did it live up to my expectations? 👍 👎 Why? _____

_____

My overall rating ☀ ☀ ☀ ☀ ☀ Do it again? 👍 👎

87

BUCKET LIST ITEM

_____
_____

I want to do this because

_____

——— I CAN CHECK IT OFF THE LIST! ———

The date I nailed it _____

Where the magic happened _____

The Story _____
_____
_____
_____
_____
_____
_____
_____
_____

My Best Memories _____
_____
_____
_____

Did it live up to my expectations? 👍 👎 Why? _____
_____
_____

My overall rating ☀ ☀ ☀ ☀ ☀ Do it again? 👍 👎

88

BUCKET LIST ITEM

_____

_____

I want to do this because

_____

— I CAN CHECK IT OFF THE LIST! —

The date I nailed it _____

Where the magic happened _____

The Story _____

_____

_____

_____

_____

_____

_____

_____

_____

My Best Memories _____

_____

_____

_____

_____

Did it live up to my expectations? 👍 👎 Why?_____

_____

_____

My overall rating ☀ ☀ ☀ ☀ ☀ Do it again? 👍 👎

89

BUCKET LIST ITEM

_____

_____

I want to do this because

_____

— I CAN CHECK IT OFF THE LIST! —

The date I nailed it _____

Where the magic happened _____

The Story _____

_____

_____

_____

_____

_____

_____

_____

My Best Memories _____

_____

_____

_____

Did it live up to my expectations? 👍 👎 Why? _____

_____

_____

My overall rating ☀ ☀ ☀ ☀ ☀ Do it again? 👍 👎

90

BUCKET LIST ITEM

_____
_____

I want to do this because
_____
_____

―――――― I CAN CHECK IT OFF THE LIST! ――――――

The date I nailed it _____

Where the magic happened _____

The Story _____
_____
_____
_____
_____
_____
_____
_____
_____
_____
_____

My Best Memories _____
_____
_____
_____
_____

Did it live up to my expectations? 👍 👎 Why? _____
_____

My overall rating ☀ ☀ ☀ ☀ ☀ Do it again? 👍 👎

91

BUCKET LIST ITEM

_____

_____

I want to do this because

_____

_____

———— I CAN CHECK IT OFF THE LIST! ————

The date I nailed it _____

Where the magic happened _____

The Story _____

_____

_____

_____

_____

_____

_____

_____

_____

My Best Memories _____

_____

_____

_____

Did it live up to my expectations? 👍 👎 Why?_____

_____

_____

My overall rating ☀ ☀ ☀ ☀ ☀ Do it again? 👍 👎

92

BUCKET LIST ITEM

_____

_____

I want to do this because

_____

———— I CAN CHECK IT OFF THE LIST! ————

The date I nailed it _____

Where the magic happened _____

The Story _____

_____

_____

_____

_____

_____

_____

_____

_____

_____

My Best Memories _____

_____

_____

_____

_____

Did it live up to my expectations? 👍 👎 Why?_____

_____

_____

My overall rating ☀ ☀ ☀ ☀ ☀ Do it again? 👍 👎

93

BUCKET LIST ITEM

_____

_____

I want to do this because

_____

_____

————— I CAN CHECK IT OFF THE LIST! —————

The date I nailed it _____

Where the magic happened _____

The Story _____

_____

_____

_____

_____

_____

_____

_____

My Best Memories _____

_____

_____

_____

Did it live up to my expectations? 👍 👎 Why? _____

_____

My overall rating ☀ ☀ ☀ ☀ ☀ Do it again? 👍 👎

94

BUCKET LIST ITEM

_____
_____

I want to do this because

_____

——— I CAN CHECK IT OFF THE LIST! ———

The date I nailed it _____

Where the magic happened _____

The Story _____
_____
_____
_____
_____
_____
_____
_____
_____
_____

My Best Memories _____
_____
_____
_____
_____

Did it live up to my expectations? 👍 👎 Why?_____

_____

My overall rating ☀ ☀ ☀ ☀ ☀ Do it again? 👍 👎

95

BUCKET LIST ITEM

I want to do this because

─── I CAN CHECK IT OFF THE LIST! ───

The date I nailed it

Where the magic happened

The Story

My Best Memories

Did it live up to my expectations? 👍 👎 Why?

My overall rating ☀ ☀ ☀ ☀ ☀ Do it again? 👍 👎

96

BUCKET LIST ITEM

_____

_____

I want to do this because

_____

—————— I CAN CHECK IT OFF THE LIST! ——————

The date I nailed it _____

Where the magic happened _____

The Story _____

_____

_____

_____

_____

_____

_____

_____

_____

_____

_____

My Best Memories _____

_____

_____

_____

Did it live up to my expectations? 👍 👎 Why? _____

_____

_____

My overall rating ☀ ☀ ☀ ☀ ☀ Do it again? 👍 👎

97

BUCKET LIST ITEM

_____

_____

I want to do this because

_____

_____

— **I CAN CHECK IT OFF THE LIST!** —

The date I nailed it _____

Where the magic happened _____

The Story _____

_____

_____

_____

_____

_____

_____

_____

_____

My Best Memories _____

_____

_____

_____

Did it live up to my expectations? 👍 👎 Why? _____

_____

_____

My overall rating ☀ ☀ ☀ ☀ ☀ Do it again? 👍 👎

98

BUCKET LIST ITEM

_____

_____

I want to do this because

_____

_____

——— I CAN CHECK IT OFF THE LIST! ———

The date I nailed it _____

Where the magic happened _____

The Story _____

_____

_____

_____

_____

_____

_____

_____

_____

_____

_____

My Best Memories _____

_____

_____

_____

_____

Did it live up to my expectations? 👍 👎 Why?_____

_____

My overall rating ☀ ☀ ☀ ☀ ☀ Do it again? 👍 👎

99

BUCKET LIST ITEM

_____

_____

I want to do this because

_____

— I CAN CHECK IT OFF THE LIST! —

The date I nailed it _____

Where the magic happened _____

The Story _____

_____

_____

_____

_____

_____

_____

_____

My Best Memories _____

_____

_____

_____

Did it live up to my expectations? 👍 👎 Why?_____

_____

My overall rating ☀ ☀ ☀ ☀ ☀ Do it again? 👍 👎

100

BUCKET LIST ITEM
_____
_____

I want to do this because
_____

_____ I CAN CHECK IT OFF THE LIST! _____

The date I nailed it _____

Where the magic happened _____

The Story _____
_____
_____
_____
_____
_____
_____
_____
_____
_____

My Best Memories _____
_____
_____
_____
_____

Did it live up to my expectations? Why?_____
_____
_____

My overall rating 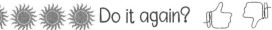 Do it again?

Made in the USA
Monee, IL
30 December 2022